POP CULTURE BIOS

ACTION MOVIE STARS

BOOBOO STEWART

TWILIGHT'S BREAKOUT IDOL

MARCIA AMIDON LUSTED

Lerner Publications Company

MINNEAPOLIS

Lerner Publications Company
A division of Lerner Publishing Group, Inc.
241 First Avenue North
Minneapolis, MN 55401 U.S.A.

Website address: www.lernerbooks.com

Library of Congress Cataloging-in-Publication Data

Lusted, Marcia Amidon.
    Booboo Stewart : Twilight's breakout idol / by Marcia
Amidon Lusted.
        p.   cm. — (Pop culture bios: action movie stars)
    Includes index.
    ISBN 978-1-4677-0746-6 (lib. bdg. : alk. paper)
    1. Stewart, Boo Boo, Juvenile literature. 2. Actors—United
States—Biography—Juvenile literature. 3. Singers—United
States—Biography—Juvenile literature. I. Title.
PN2287.S6788L86 2013
791.4302'8092—dc23 [B]   2012020039

Manufactured in the United States of America
1 – PC – 12/31/12

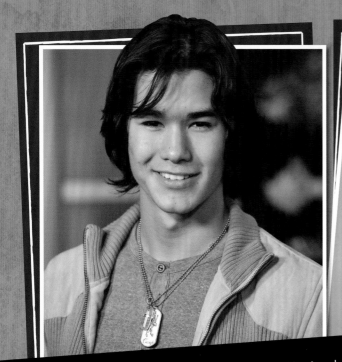

INTRODUCTION

In 2009, Booboo Stewart got a life-changing phone call. His agent was on the other end of the line. The agent told him that an audition he'd been on had gone well—very well, in fact! The audition was for *Eclipse*, the third of five films based on Stephenie Meyer's *Twilight* books. The film's director, David Slade, was so impressed with Booboo that he wanted him to play Seth Clearwater, the young part human, part wolf who helps protect main character Bella Swan from an evil vampire.

AGENT =
a businessperson who helps actors find work

Booboo cut his hair short to play the character Seth Clearwater in 2009.

Booboo was thrilled! Playing Seth would do amazing things for his career. Yet he also took the news in stride. "My first reaction was a lot of yelling, screaming, and running around," Booboo recalls. "Then my mom made me go and do yard work." Booboo's family always *has* been pretty down-to-earth!

Booboo (SECOND FROM LEFT) poses with his fellow *Eclipse* cast members and director David Slade (CENTER FRONT) at the London premiere of the movie in 2010.

Besides, as exciting as it was to get the part, Booboo was no stranger to films, TV, and even the music scene. He'd been a big name long before the Twilight opportunity had come around. For Booboo, acting in a Twilight film was just one more awesome thing in a long line of accomplishments that have made him a huge fav with fans everywhere!

Booboo offers a friendly smile while holding court on the red carpet.

Booboo with his parents and sister Fivel in 2007

CHAPTER ONE

CALI KID

Booboo with his sister Fivel (LEFT) and model Kathy Ireland at a charity event in 2004.

Just who is Booboo Stewart and what's his story? This supertalented guy was born on January 21, 1994, in Beverly Hills, California. His parents named him Nils Allen Stewart Jr., after his dad, but they soon started calling him Booboo. Booboo explains the origins of his nickname this way: "When I was a baby, I always used to suck my two fingers, and my parents said I had a boo boo face." (By "boo boo face," they meant a pouty or sad-looking expression.) "That's how I got my name!" The name has stuck for all these years.

Booboo has three sisters, none of whom has any unusual nicknames. His sisters Fivel and Maegan are older than him. Sister Sage is younger. The sibs all have dark hair and dark eyes. They are a mix of Chinese, Japanese, and Korean from their mom's side and Russian, Scottish, and Blackfoot American Indian from their dad's side.

Booboo with his sisters Fivel (LEFT), Maegan (RIGHT), and Sage (FRONT) in 2011.

Booboo and his sisters were homeschooled. Booboo also was in GATE, a program for gifted students. He finished high school early by completing his lessons on a computer program that he could use anywhere, even on planes and movie sets.

Early Start

Booboo has been in show biz for years. He got his start onstage by learning martial arts when he was three. He often practiced martial arts in front of a crowd. In 2002 and 2003, he won the Junior Martial Arts World Championship. He earned a black belt—the highest rank you can earn in martial arts. In 2004, Booboo made the Martial Arts Junior Hall of Fame. That was an epic achievement for someone who was only ten!

Booboo's martial arts training helped him break into show business. He began by doing stunt work for TV shows. "I started doing stunts; then, slowly, I just started acting," Booboo explained.

MARTIAL ARTS =
<u>forms of self-defense</u>
<u>that are often</u>
<u>practiced as sports</u>

Booboo shows off his martial arts moves in 2007.

In 2004, Booboo made appearances in the TV show *Big Time*. Then he got a part in the film *Yard Sale*. Between 2004 and 2010, Booboo had parts in more than twenty films and TV shows! He did stunt work for the films *Zoom* and *Beowulf*. "We did wire works," Booboo said. Wire works are stunts that actors perform with wires attached to their bodies for support—for instance, they might do a flip while wires hold their arms and legs in place to keep them from slipping. "I had to do a scene where I had to run up this guy and spin. It was really fun. It was a little crazy!" Booboo recalled.

Booboo performed stunt work in the movie *Beowulf*.

Making Music

In addition to acting, Booboo has a passion for music. He's loved to sing since he was little. He also plays the guitar, the piano, and the drums.

FROM LEFT: Jade Gilley, Booboo, Miki Ishikawa, and Taylor McKinney made music as members of T-Squad.

In 2006, Booboo learned that singer Vitamin C was holding tryouts for a Radio Disney music group called T-Squad. T-Squad (which was active from 2006 to 2008) would make fun, upbeat pop and hip-hop music for kids. Booboo was all over that opportunity! He tried out for Vitamin C and made the cut. So did dancer Jade Gilley, actress Miki Ishikawa, and rapper Taylor McKinney. The group released an album in 2007.

Booboo had some of his first experiences with crazed fans as a member of T-Squad. "I was at a football game one time, and when we were walking away, we had to run like crazy 'cuz all these fans had my arm!" he said.

BOOBOO'S FAVORITE BAND

Booboo loves the band Boston. This group was really popular in the 1970s and the 1980s. Songs by this band include "More Than a Feeling," "Rock and Roll Band," and "Amanda."

"They were trying to rip my arm off, and we were running and running."

Booboo's music career was just getting started with T-Squad. He soon started touring with other Radio Disney acts, including the Cheetah Girls and Miley Cyrus. He also filmed a commercial for Miley. He reports that she is super nice. Booboo sang two songs for the Walt Disney Company too. One was the theme for the 2008 Disney Channel Games. The other was a song for the *DisneyMania 7* album. Finally, Booboo started a band with his sisters Maegan and Fivel called TSC (The Stewart Clan). They toured together for a while, but these days, it's just Fivel and Booboo who sing together. They've even recorded their own album together called *Change*.

Booboo plays guitar while Fivel sings backup during a performance in 2008.

CHAPTER TWO

MAKIN' IT

Booboo stands next to one of his modeling posters in 2012.

Booboo speaks at an event to help kids with muscular dystrophy in 2010.

Believe it or not, Booboo had still other goals in addition to acting and singing. He hoped to get more publicity for himself by doing some modeling. That plan worked out well for him. He was soon the most in-demand model under the age of eighteen! He also wrote and illustrated a comic book called *Millennium Man*. It was about a character he'd made up when he was twelve.

PUBLICITY = public attention. Stars work hard to gain publicity for themselves to help advance their careers.

Giving Back

Along with helping his career, Booboo was very interested in helping others. He'd always been touched by the hardships people face when they're diagnosed with a disease. So in 2010, he became an ambassador for the Muscular Dystrophy Association. He appeared in ads for its "Make a Muscle, Make a Difference" campaign.

AMBASSADOR = spokesperson

Booboo and Fivel serve a meal at the Los Angeles Mission in 2011.

Booboo and his sister Fivel also supported the Los Angeles Mission. It's a place where homeless people can go to find food and shelter. Booboo and Fivel often went to the mission to serve meals to the homeless. In 2010 and 2011, Booboo went to Australia to be in a telethon. It was to raise money for a hospital. Booboo even took his shirt off and showed off his awesome abs to raise more money! The telethon raised more than $13 million.

Booboo shows off his abs at the beach.

The Big Screen Gets Bigger

Booboo was getting the chance to appear in even bigger films too. His name was spreading among Hollywood bigwigs. At the age of fifteen, Booboo got the most epic career news of all. He was offered the role of Seth Clearwater in *Eclipse*. This role catapulted Booboo into superstardom.

CHAPTER THREE

TWILIGHT TIME

Booboo with long hair in 2009

Hi Boo Boo! Welcome to The "Twilight" Family

xxoo, twifans.com & cullenboysanonymous.com

Booboo meets a couple of Twilight fans in 2009.

After being cast as Seth, Booboo threw himself into the role completely. He knew the part would take a lot of commitment—not only because Seth is important to the *Eclipse* story but also because the character shows up again in the fourth and fifth Twilight movies. Booboo had signed on to be in all three films.

Fortunately, Booboo felt a kinship with the character right away. Like Seth, Booboo is easygoing. He believes in being kind to everyone and in helping others. Yet there was one thing about playing Seth that Booboo didn't like. Booboo's hair was long, and Seth's is closely cropped. This meant Booboo needed to get a major haircut!

Booboo in a scene from *Eclipse*

HEALTH NUT

Booboo tries to live a healthful lifestyle. He eats healthful foods and goes to the gym six times a week. He also loves outdoor exercise.

"My hair was so long, it was at my shoulders," Booboo remarked. "Then they said that I had to cut it. It was crazy having my hair so short! It hasn't been that short since I was nine." Still, Booboo managed to adjust to his new do.

Seth as a Fighter

As easygoing as Seth is, the character does take part in fights. He changes from boy to wolf to do battle against vampires. People often ask Booboo what it was like to do the fight scenes. After all, he's great at doing film stunts and he likes the challenge they present. But Booboo always explains that he really didn't participate in the fight scenes for *Eclipse*. Since Seth fights in wolf form, those scenes were filmed using CGI.

CGI =
computer-generated imagery. CGI is used to create scenes that can't be filmed using real actors.

Booboo with actress Julia Jones in *Breaking Dawn Part 1*

"I wish I had been a part of the scenes, though," Booboo admitted. "It would have been really fun!"

Familiar Story

Booboo knew the story in the Twilight books inside and out because he'd read them all closely before auditioning for the part. He loved all four books and felt a deep connection with the characters.

Booboo read the entire Twilight series to prepare for his audition.

He even got to meet and talk with Twilight author Stephenie Meyer. She had a cameo in the fourth Twilight film. "She sits right in front of me in one scene, and that was the first time I had really spoken to her and got to know her. She is really nice, down-to-earth," he dished. Booboo also loved connecting with his fellow actors. "It was really fun filming and working with [the other actors]," he stated. "It was really cool to be hanging around with them."

Booboo was sad when Twilight filming ended. He'd miss seeing his Twilight friends every day.

CAMEO =
a brief appearance by a well-known person in a film or TV show

Stephenie Meyer, author of the Twilight series

Booboo hangs out with fellow Twilight werewolves Taylor Lautner (LEFT) and Alex Meraz (RIGHT) at the 2010 Teen Choice Awards.

But he was also excited about his post-Twilight life. He couldn't be more grateful for the chance to be a part of the project. "Being a part of Twilight has given me a bigger opportunity for more projects, and it lets me do the things that I want to do," he explained. "It's been awesome. Most of us will probably never do a movie *this* big in our life, so it's really exciting."

VARIETY IS GOOD!

Booboo's favorite thing about being a film actor is that he gets to play different people. He thinks it would get boring after a while to always play the same person.

Booboo (LEFT) and Fivel (RIGHT) perform with their band, 5L, in April 2012.

CHAPTER FOUR

THE FUTURE

FROM LEFT: Twilight actors Elizabeth Reaser, Ashley Greene, Nikki Reed, Julia Jones, and Booboo attend Comic Con in San Diego, California, in 2011.

Even with the Twilight films behind him, Booboo still has tons of work on his plate. Immediately after Twilight, he acted in a 2012 film called *White Frog*. It's the story of a kid named Nick who has Asperger's syndrome. Booboo plays Nick.

When Booboo went to audition for *White Frog*, he knew it wasn't a blockbuster movie like the Twilight films. But he thought the script and the character of Nick were great. "It was a once in a lifetime opportunity," he said. Yet playing Nick was hard. "Every day I'd come off set and I'd just fall asleep in the car," Booboo said. "My brain has never hurt that much in my whole entire life."

ASPERGER'S SYNDROME = a disorder that affects a person's social skills. People with Asperger's syndrome might not pick up on social cues and may have a hard time communicating.

Harry Schum Jr. (LEFT) and Tyler Posey (RIGHT) also star in *White Frog*.

Still, Booboo also reportedly said that the set of *White Frog* was the happiest set he'd ever been on! He had tons of fun working with his fellow cast members, and he made lots of friends.

Life Offscreen

On top of *White Frog*, Booboo has a lot going on offscreen. He lives in L.A. with his family, and he makes sure to set aside plenty of time to spend with them. The Stewarts love hanging out together! The family also keeps busy caring for their many pets. The Stewart family has several dogs, a cat, and horses. Booboo says his house is like a petting zoo!

Booboo also often teams up with big sis Fivel to make music. They even started a YouTube channel to showcase their music and other projects.

Booboo and Fivel perform as the band 5L with Ryan Cook (LEFT) and Davin Baltazar (RIGHT).

And in the fall of 2011, the sibs came together again for a different venture. They became ambassadors for Four Green Steps, a company that sells Earth-friendly products. Both Booboo and Fivel are into being "green."

Looking Ahead

What does the future hold for Booboo? No one can say for sure. After all, he has so many talents, there's just no telling what he'll do next! Whatever he does, there's little doubt he'll succeed. For now, he's just enjoying the ride. "It is so much fun being able to be in this business where I get to do what I really want to do," he says. "And the best advice I can give to other kids is just never give up. You have to keep on trying."

BOOBOO
PICS!

Booboo and Fivel at the 2012 MTV Movie Awards

Booboo at the premiere of Breaking Dawn Part 1

SOURCE NOTES

6   Brooke Hunter and Morgan Sutherland, "BooBoo Stewart Interview as Seth Clearwater in Twilight Saga Breaking Dawn," *Girl.com.au,* n.d., http://www.girl.com.au/booboo-stewart-twilight-saga-breaking-dawn-interview.htm (May 30, 2012).

9   Sindy, "Boo Boo Stewart Interview," *Kidzworld.com,* n.d., http://www.kidzworld.com/article/10021-boo-boo-stewart-interview (May 30, 2012).

10   Hunter and Sutherland, "BooBoo Stewart Interview."

11   Sindy, "Boo Boo Stewart Interview."

12-13   Ibid.

20   Hunter and Sutherland, "BooBoo Stewart Interview."

21   Ibid.

22   Ibid.

22   Ibid.

23   Melody Lee, "Winter Issue Extra: Booboo Stewart," *Audrey Magazine,* January 18, 2012, http://audreymagazine.com/winter-issue-extra-booboo-stewart/ (June 4, 2012).

25   Melody Lee, "Boy Wonder: Booboo Stewart," *Audrey Magazine,* March 21, 2012, http://audreymagazine.com/personalities-boy-wonder-booboo-stewart/ (June 4, 2012).

25   Lee, "Winter Issue Extra: Booboo Stewart."

27   Hunter and Sutherland, "BooBoo Stewart Interview."

27   Tai, "Exclusive Booboo Stewart Interview," QuileuteWolfPack.com, July 2, 2010, http://quileutewolfpack.com/newsblog/?p=8540 (June 8, 2012).

MORE BOOBOO INFO

Booboo and Fivel Stewart
http://www.boobooandfivel.com
Fans won't want to miss this website of celebrity sibs Booboo and Fivel Stewart. Here you'll find blog posts by Booboo and Fivel, videos and music, and official bios.

IMDb: Booboo Stewart
http://www.imdb.com/name/nm1559927
Visit Booboo's Internet Movie Database page to see pictures of the star, a complete list of films and TV shows he's been in, and a brief biography.

Landau, Elaine. *Taylor Lautner: Twilight's Fearless Werewolf.* Minneapolis: Lerner Publications Company, 2013. Twilight fans will adore this bio packed with info on Taylor Lautner and the film series that turned both Taylor and Booboo into instant superstars.

Meyer, Stephenie. *The Twilight Saga: The Official Illustrated Guide.* New York: Little, Brown, and Co., 2011. Want to learn more about Seth Clearwater—or anything else related to Twilight? Look no further than this extensive guide.

The Twilight Saga
http://thetwilightsaga.com
Read up on all things Twilight at this site especially for Twihards.

INDEX

PHOTO ACKNOWLEDGMENTS

The images in this book are used with the permission of: © Michael Kovac/Stringer/Getty Images, p. 2; © Brad Washburn/Film Magic/Getty Images, pp. 3 (top), 8 (left); © Frazer Harrison/Getty Images, pp. 3 (bottom), 18 (bottom/left); © Featureflash/Dreamstime.com, p. 4 (top/left); Picture Perfect/Rex USA, p. 4 (top/right); AP Photo/Invision/Jordan Strauss, p. 4 (bottom); © Kevin Winter/Getty Images, p. 5; © Dave Hogan/Getty Images, pp. 6, 18 (top); © Jon Furniss/WireImage/Getty Images, p. 7; © Michael Tullberg/Getty Images, p. 8 (right); © Jeffrey Mayer/WireImage/Getty Images, p. 9; © Smith/Retna Ltd./CORBIS, p. 11 (top); Paramount/Shangri-La/Kobal Collection/Art Resource, NY, p. 11 (bottom); © Chad Buchanan/Getty Images, p. 12; © Alberto E. Rodriguez/Getty Images, p. 13; BSA/ZOJ WENN Photos/Newscom, p. 14 (bottom); © Ethan Miller/Getty Images, p. 14 (top); © Gabriel Olsen/Film Magic/Getty Images, p. 16 (top); © Splash News/CORBIS, pp. 16 (bottom), 24 (bottom); Mary Evans/Walt Disney/Pixar/Courtesy Everett Collection, p. 17; © Eric Charbonneau/WireImage/Getty Images, p. 18 (bottom/right); © A.F. Archive/Alamy, p. 19; RK/WENN Photos/Newscom, p. 20; © Archives du 7e Art/Summit Entertainment/Photos 12/Alamy, p. 21 (top); © Todd Strand/Independent Picture Service, p. 21 (bottom); Matt Baron/BEImages/Rex USA, p. 22; © Kevin Winter/TCA 2010/Getty Images for TCA, p. 23; © Jen Lowery/Splash News/CORBIS, p. 24 (top); © Paul Archuleta/Film Magic/Getty Images, p. 25; © Paul A. Herbet/Film Magic/Getty Images, pp. 26, 29 (top/middle); © Michael Kovac/Stringer/Getty Images, p. 27; © Tibrina Hobson/Getty Images, p. 28 (top/left); © Alexandra Wyman/WireImage/Getty Images, p. 28 (right); © Christopher Polk/Getty Images, p. 28 (bottom/left); Sthanlee B. Mirador/Pacific Rim Photo Press/Newscom, p. 29 (top/left); © Jon Kopaloff/FilmMagic/Getty Images, p. 29 (right); © Gregg DeGuire/FilmMagic/Getty Images, p. 29 (bottom).

Front Cover: TLeopold/Globe-ZUMA/Newscom (main); © Gregg DeGuire/FilmMagic/Getty Images. Back cover: Albert L. Ortega/PictureGroup/AP Images.

Main body text set in Shannon Std Book 12/18.
Typeface provided by Monotype Typography.